Photo Album,
page 43

Crafting with nature in a Weekend

Dorothy Wood

David & Charles

A DAVID & CHARLES BOOK

First published in the UK in 2004

Copyright © Dorothy Wood 2004

Distributed in North America
by F&W Publications, Inc.
4700 East Galbraith Road
Cincinnati, OH 45236
1-800-289-0963

A catalogue record for this book is available
from the British Library.

ISBN 0 7153 1710 5 hardback
ISBN 0 7153 1711 3 paperback

Executive Editor CHERYL BROWN
Desk Editor JENNIFER PROVERBS
Executive Art Editor ALI MYER
Senior Designer LISA FORRESTER
Production Controller ROS NAPPER
Photographer SIMON WHITMORE

Printed in China by Hong Kong Graphics & Printing Ltd.
for David & Charles
Brunel House   Newton Abbot Devon

Visit our website at
www.davidandcharles.co.uk

David & Charles books are available from
all good book shops; alternatively you can
contact our Orderline on (0)1626 334555
or write to us at FREEPOST EX2 110, David
& Charles Direct, Newton Abbot, TQ12 4ZZ
(no stamp required UK mainland).

The author and publisher have made every
effort to ensure that all the instructions
in this book are accurate and safe, and
therefore cannot accept liability for any
resulting injury, damage or loss to persons
or property however it may arise.

CONTENTS

INTRODUCTION

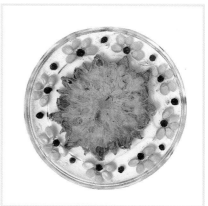

Most good craft shops stock a huge variety of natural materials. Along their shelves you can find bags of moss in a range of colours, interesting pieces of lichen, bundles of willow branches, boxes full of exquisite sea shells, sliced dried fruits, skeleton leaves and lots of gorgeous exotic things from around the world. This wonderful resource of materials is just what you need to make the beautiful projects in this book.

Of course it is also possible to collect your own natural materials – pine cones and acorns from the woods, shells and driftwood from the beach and flowers from the garden. Before you begin to gather your materials it is worth reading through the technical section (pages 6–18) because there are lots of tips as well as helpful information about collecting, preparing and storing natural materials, quick ways of preserving products such as flowers, sliced fruit and seed heads and advice about the different glues you can use.

For easy reference the projects and ideas are divided into five groups, each using materials from a different environment: the beach, garden, kitchen, woodland and exotic locations. You may find that you already have many of the materials needed for some of the projects – perhaps you have some interesting pieces found on your last beach holiday, some dried pulses in the kitchen cupboard, or even whole nuts left over from Christmas.

Remember that the clear step-by-step instructions are only a starting point – you can use whatever materials you like for a particular project. For example, change the woodland wreath into a summer decoration covered in shells, or use little pieces of sea glass to make a door plaque for a beach house. The possibilities are endless and the only boundaries are in your imagination.

MATERIALS AND EQUIPMENT

There is nothing particularly specialized about the materials and equipment for making the projects in this book. Unless you are an absolute beginner you will probably already have some of the things you need, and no doubt if you do have to buy anything new you will be able to reuse it for other crafting projects. Listed here are some of the most frequently used tools and equipment along with any items that need further explanation.

MATERIALS

Self-hardening clay is available from craft shops and comes in brown or white. It is easy to roll and mould. Natural products can be inset into the clay, imprinted or glued in place once it has dried.

Crystal resin is required for the Fruit Coasters (page 90) but is generally used for making small paperweights. The clear resin is mixed with a hardener and poured over the item(s) to be suspended in it. It takes several hours to dry.

Mosaic grout is much finer than ordinary ready-mixed grout and is ideal for giving a smooth finish to small mosaic materials such as eggshell (see Eggshell Mosaic, page 70). Apply mosaic grout with care (see page 17).

Imitation gold leaf and gilding wax add a festive or luxurious touch to natural materials (see the Golden Nut Tree, page 74 and right). Seal the leaf metal with shellac to prevent tarnishing.

Glue is used to bond a variety of materials, and the appropriate type you will need is listed with each project. Those glues used in this book include craft glue, which is suitable for many applications; silicone

glue and the hot-glue gun (see picture, above) for when a strong, clear adhesive is required; and two-way glue, which dries tacky and can be used for repositioning or to attach imitation gold leaf (see the Oriental Lamp Base, page 84). For a guide to using glue, see Working with Glues, opposite.

Mod Podge, shellac and **polyurethane varnish** can all be used to seal, protect and add sheen to the finished projects. The product you use will depend on the materials you have and the type of finish you require. Choose matt, gloss or satin finishes.

Perspex strips (clear acrylic) are ideal for the sides of moulds when using plaster. The type used for picture framing is easy to cut and can be reused indefinitely.

Plaster of paris is a white powder that is mixed with water to make a hard white earthenware-type material. Arrange natural materials on top before it sets (see Beach Memories Plaque, page 24) or pour the plaster into a mould over the design (see Miniature-shell Tiles, page 20).

Plasticine (moulding clay) is a non-drying clay that is an ideal base on which you can arrange natural material to make a design in a mould. It can be rinsed, dried and reused. Note that the part of the material sunk into the plasticine will be the part that shows on the finished design when the plasticine in pulled away.

Waxes for finishing are used to seal and colour the wooden bases of some of the featured projects. They come in many forms that can add sheen, colour or a particular finish. Patinating wax is a specialized coloured wax that makes an item look aged.

WORKING WITH GLUES

There are many different glues, most of which have been designed for a particular task.

Bonding glass to glass as on the Sea-glass Candleholder (page 30) requires a strong, high-tack glue that dries clear. This glue will hold the pieces securely for grouting and allow the light to shine through when the project is finished.

Rough materials such as pine cones, acorns or rosebuds should be glued to a surface with silicone adhesive. Use a clear silicone adhesive if the glue will be visible once the mosaic is complete. Silicone adhesive for bathroom tiles is an inexpensive option for a large project or use small tubes of adhesive sold for découpage.

Curved surfaces are difficult to glue, but a hot-glue gun works well because the glue sets almost instantly. Do not use a hot-glue gun with some plastics or polystyrene shapes because the heat will melt them.

Upright surfaces such as the Oriental Lamp Base (page 84) can also be difficult. Use a type of glue that dries very quickly and has a high tack such as extra-strong PVA (white) glue.

EQUIPMENT

Brushes of various types are needed for applying paint, varnish and glue. They should be cleaned immediately after use with the appropriate solvent. If there is a short gap as you work on a project, leave the brush soaking in cleaning solution. Keep separate brushes for glue.

Craft knife/vegetable knife with a very firm blade is ideal for cutting natural materials. Change craft-knife blades often before they become blunt. Always cut away from yourself and use a cutting mat to protect your work surface.

Cutting mat (self-healing) is useful for rolling out clay and measuring materials as well as for cutting. Keep one side for cutting and turn over for rolling clay.

Flower presses of the traditional type are fine but microwave flower presses speed up the process of pressing flowers significantly. (See page 16).

Latex gloves are invaluable for protecting your hands from chemicals or rough natural products and to keep them clean when using paints, varnishes and waxes.

Masking tape will hold glued pieces in position while they dry.

Measuring jugs/spoons are essential for measuring precise amounts. You may need a container that can measure small amounts as well as the type of standard measuring jug used in the kitchen.

Mixing bowls/containers should be old or disposable because you are dealing with plaster, resin and grout. Scrape out the containers after use and avoid washing leftover mixed material in the sink – you could cause a blockage.

Pencil/marker pen is required for marking shapes and measurements. Make sure that the marks can either be removed or hidden on completion.

Rolling pins in wood or plastic are ideal for clay. Remember to wash rolling pins thoroughly after use before they are used for food purposes again. Even better, keep one specifically for this purpose.

Secateurs with sharp blades and a lever action make it easy to cut wood and pine cones.

Tape measures and **rulers** are not interchangeable. Use a tape measure for curved surfaces and a ruler for measuring or marking straight lines. Metal safety rulers are essential for cutting with a craft knife.

Tweezers are indispensable for moving or arranging small pieces of natural material. Keep the grabbing surfaces free from glue.

BLANKS AND FORMS

These are used for a number of projects in this book including the Summer Flowers Clock (page 34) and the Winter Leaf Tray (page 40).

Dry foam or polystyrene in the form of wreaths, balls and other more unusual shapes can be covered with natural materials. Choose the adhesive to suit both the base and the natural material. These are obtainable from craft shops and some florists.

Papier mâché is inexpensive and surprisingly sturdy. You can buy blanks in a range of sizes and shapes or try making your own. The item can be painted or covered to suit the design. (See the Bridal Keepsakes Box, page 44.)

Wood is an ideal base for natural craft projects, being a natural product itself. Wooden blanks range from boxes to picture frames and trays. Finish the wood with wax, varnish or paint for different effects.

TECHNIQUES

Although each project in this book has detailed step-by-step instructions that will allow you to complete it, they do assume some previous knowledge. There isn't room to explain the basics every time and this chapter aims to fill the gap. It provides information on how to collect, prepare and store natural materials, gives advice on the different glues suitable, and includes detailed instructions on using plaster and grout.

COLLECTING AND STORING NATURAL MATERIAL

Collecting your own shells, pine cones, flowers and other natural materials is rewarding and satisfying, particularly when you can turn them into a gift or lasting memento, and you have the pleasure of knowing you took the project through from start to finish. However, it isn't easy to get the quantity and quality required and you may want to make something when the materials aren't available. When you buy them from a shop you can be sure of getting exactly the right size, colour and shape for your project, and you will be able to buy more if needed. Purchased items will also have been prepared so that they are clean, dry, safe and ready to use.

If you are lucky enough to have access to a source of natural material, whether permanently or while on holiday, take the opportunity to collect some supplies for future use. Of course, finding particular natural materials is not guaranteed all year round – there are no acorns in the middle of summer and it is difficult to find flowers to press or preserve in the middle of winter. The secret is to collect when something is available and then dry and store carefully so that it is in peak condition when you come to make your natural project.

There are so many different natural materials suitable for the projects shown in this book, that it would be impossible to give information on how to treat everything you might use. However, the guidelines above right will come in useful at this first stage.

For best results when collecting and storing natural material...

■ Collect flowers and leaves when their colour and shape are at their peak

■ Look for bright colours because it is inevitable that some fading will occur

■ Collect plant material in paper bags until you have the opportunity to preserve it – a polythene bag retains moisture and items inside will go mouldy

■ Pick plant material mid morning when it is dry so that there is no dew or moisture on it

■ The worst time to gather flowers is at noon as they have too much moisture in them; place in a vase for about an hour so they can evaporate slightly

■ Once you have collected the material, begin the drying process as soon as possible

■ Store dried material in a dry area away from high humidity or direct sunlight

CLEANING AND PREPARING NATURAL MATERIAL

Some natural materials may appear to be ready to use straight away, but it is worth spending a little time on preparation to make sure they don't go

mouldy or disintegrate once a project is completed. Some materials, such as shells collected from the beach or pine cones from the forest, may appear quite inert, but even these will require some preparation before use. Soaking non-porous objects in a weak solution of bleach or boiling in water sterilizes them and kills off the bacteria that causes mould and smells. Other materials can be heated in an oven.

For best results when preparing material...

■ Prepare pine cones by spreading them out on parchment or foil and baking them at a low heat. This dries the cones and kills any insects inside.

■ Remove animal tissue from live seashells by boiling for a few minutes and then pulling it out with tweezers. You can also immerse the shells in water and freeze overnight. Allow the shells to thaw and remove the animal tissue as above.

■ Clean empty seashells and previously live seashells in a 50:50 solution of bleach and water. Leave the shell until the periostracum is gone (the flaky, leathery skin that covers most live seashells).

■ Boil eggshells. This thickens the membrane, making it easier to remove. It also sterilizes the shells and prevents them going mouldy.

DRYING AND PRESERVING NATURAL MATERIAL

Flowers, leaves and other fresh natural materials need to be dried to preserve their colour and shape. There are a number of different methods of doing this: heating, hanging, using silica gel and pressing. Choose the one that best suits your materials and the time you have available. If you are planning ahead and collecting items that are in season, then time is not an issue, but when you want to prepare your material and make your project in a weekend you need to choose a quick method. Having said that, drying plant material as quickly as possible helps best preserve the colour and shape. One way to speed the process of drying is to use a microwave oven (see opposite). You can use a microwave to dry materials in a number of ways but one of the most beneficial is pressing (page 16).

HEATING

Materials: pine cones, fruit slices, chillies and other items

For best results...

■ Use a low heat of 100° C (200° F) or less

■ If your oven is fan-assisted, leave the door open to circulate the air as the material dries

■ Lay pine cones out on baking parchment and leave in the oven for about 3–4 hours until they have opened

■ When drying pine cones do not overheat because the pine pitch can ignite

■ Watch the natural material carefully as it begins to dry – fruit slices in particular can turn dark brown very quickly

Drying fruit slices in an oven

1 Cut fruit into slices 3–6mm (1/8–1/4in) thick and lay them on several sheets of absorbent paper on a baking sheet.

2 Place the tray in a low oven to dry for about 2–3 hours. Watch the fruit carefully after an hour or so and remove smaller fruits that dry more quickly.

Drying fruit slices in a microwave

1 Lay four slices of fruit on several sheets of absorbent paper and cover with another two sheets. Place the fruit in the microwave and cook on 50 per cent power for 30 seconds. Check that it hasn't scorched and change the paper if it is wet.

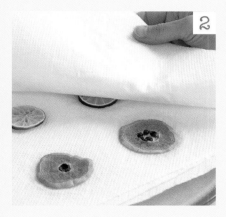

2 Continue to microwave at 50 per cent power in 30-second blasts. Turn the fruit over every minute, replacing the paper as necessary, and continue until fully dry.

Fruit Coasters, page 90

HANGING

Materials: plants and flowers that do not wilt, or don't wilt much, such as poppy seed heads, lavender and hydrangea

Time: days or weeks

For best results...

■ Remove all unnecessary foliage

■ Group stems of one type in small bundles and secure with a rubber band or string

■ Make an S-shaped hook to hang the bundles

■ Hang to dry away from direct sunlight in a warm area with good air circulation

When hanging up plant material to dry, remove unnecessary foliage and then tie your plant material in small bundles of the same type to speed the drying process.

USING SILICA GEL

Materials: roses, pansies, daisies and other flowers that are not too fleshy (tulips and crocuses are too fleshy)

Time: about a week or two, depending on the item(s)

For best results…

■ Plants dried in silica gel retain their colour and shape but are not everlasting and must be kept away from damp

■ Experiment to find the optimum times for particular sizes and shapes of flowers

■ Speed up the process by warming the gel before use, either in the oven uncovered for 10–15 minutes at 120° (250°F) or by microwaving on a medium setting

■ After use, dry the gel in the oven or microwave in the same way, then store in an airtight container for next time

■ Use an airtight container when drying with silica gel otherwise the gel will absorb moisture from the air and become saturated before your items have had a chance to dry

■ Mark the date on the container to help assess drying times

Drying flat flowers in silica gel

1

Pour about 2.5cm (1in) of silica gel into the bottom of a large, airtight container. Spoon a little mound of silica gel where each flower is to lie so that there is a 2.5–5cm (1–2in) gap between each. Place the flowers face down on top.

2

Sprinkle enough silica gel on top to cover the flowers. Fit an airtight lid and store in a dry place for 5–7 days.

3

To see if the flowers are dry, tip the box to one side or move the silica gel with a lollypop (Popsicle) stick and gently touch them. They should feel dry and papery.

Drying full flowers in silica gel

1 Pour about 2.5cm (1in) of silica gel into the bottom of a large, airtight container. Trim the stems from the flowers and sink the bottom of each flower into the gel so that none are touching.

2 Carefully add more silica gel around the flowers so that they each sit in a little mound. Use a small paintbrush to fill between any closed petals.

3 Make sure the silica gel is inside the flower head and then cover completely in silica gel. Fit an airtight lid and store in a dry place for 10–14 days. Follow step 3 for Drying Flat Flowers, below left, to check when they are dry.

Bridal Keepsakes Box,
page 44

PRESSING

Materials: most flowers and leaves except those that are very fleshy

Time: just minutes in the microwave; weeks the old-fashioned way

For best results...

■ Collect flowers mid morning on a dry day – newly opened flowers are better than older ones

■ Place flowers with a stem at the back, such as pansies and daisies, face down on the pressing mat

■ Give flowers with thick receptacles a gentle press with your finger just below the petals to flatten slightly before pressing

■ Where possible only press the same type of flower or thickness of flower on one page

■ Keep flowers and leaves well spaced during the pressing process

■ Ideally use the microwave method because it ensures minimal loss of colour and deterioration

■ Store pressed flowers between sheets of paper in a dry place

■ Keep finished projects away from direct sunlight because certain flowers, such as pansies, will fade over time

■ If you have difficulty removing a pressed flower from the fabric, you can release it slightly by stretching the fabric gently in several directions.

Using a microwave press

A microwave press is required to press plant material in a microwave but it is such an excellent little tool that you will want to use it for all sorts of projects, such as the Summer Flowers Clock (page 34) and Plaster-relief Picture (page 88). It has two plastic plates with ventilation holes, two pads, two sheets of fine cotton and clips to apply pressure as the flowers press. Wash the cotton sheets from time to time to keep them clean. The instructions here are for a 600W oven – reduce the time for higher-power ovens. Short bursts of heat allow you to check and rearrange the petals while the flower still retains some moisture.

1 Lay out one pad and piece of cotton on the flat side of a plastic plate. Trim stems from the back of flowers such as pansies and lay out face down so that there is a gap between each flower. Cover with a cotton sheet, the other pad and plate and fit the clips.

2 Place the press in the microwave and cook on full power for 40–50 seconds. Leave to rest for a moment and then cook for a further 20 seconds. Check the flowers and cook for a further 20 seconds if required. The flowers should feel papery and dry. Peel off carefully and lay on clean paper.

WORKING WITH GROUT

Where items like sea glass, seeds or eggshell have be used to create the decorative patterns on a project they can be finished with grout (see below). Ready-mixed grout or grout for tiling bathrooms is too coarse for such fine work. Use powdered grout specially designed for mosaic, which is readily available from craft shops selling mosaic tesserae.

For best results…

■ Wear protective gloves when working with grout because it is very drying to the skin. If any grout does get on your skin, rinse with vinegar to neutralize the alkalinity before washing.

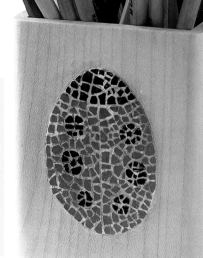

Practise grouting by making this delightful pencil box using the eggshell mosaic technique on pages 72–73, and the template on page 99. Paint the eggshell with gouache or poster paint and leave to dry before grouting (see page 73).

1

Wait until the design is set before grouting. The longer you leave it the better but allow at least 24 hours. Pour a little water into a container and mix in some powdered grout to a creamy consistency. Mix approximately 1 part of water to 2.75 parts of grout.

2

Spoon the mixed grout onto the design and smooth over the surface with your fingers. Work the grout into all the cracks and then remove as much of the excess as possible.

3

Leave to dry for a few minutes and then wipe clean with a barely damp sponge. Rinse the sponge out in clean water as you go. Leave to dry completely and then dry polish the surface of the design with a soft cloth.

WORKING WITH PLASTER

Plaster of paris is a white powder that, when mixed with water to form a thick cream, will harden to an earthenware consistency. The wet mixture can be poured onto a pattern made from natural materials that has been laid out in a mould, such as the Miniature-shell Tiles (page 20) or the materials can be dropped on top of the plaster before it sets as on the Beach Memories Plaque (page 24).

There are different grades of plaster suitable for a range of moulding projects. Basic plaster of paris is slightly coarse and is not very hard when dry. It is suitable for projects that are not subject to any wear such as the framed picture on page 88, but if you are making tiles or tablemats look out for a harder plaster such as resin plaster that is extremely fine and dries to an extra-hard finish. Different grades of plaster require slightly different proportions of water to plaster so do follow the manufacturer's guidelines. As a general rule mix the plaster and water in the proportions 100:70.

For best results...

■ When you are setting items into plaster of paris use cold water to mix up the plaster because this slows the setting process. For faster setting in a mould you can place the object in the microwave for a few seconds to speed up drying.

1 Weigh enough plaster for the project you are working on. As a rough guide, when the plaster is mixed with water it makes about 10% more volume than the dry powder alone.

2 Measure the water. Add the plaster to the water and never the other way round. Stir gently to mix and leave for a minute or two to let the air bubbles rise to the surface. Gently pour into your mould or container.

3 When working with a mould, spread the plaster into the corners with the back of a spoon to ensure that it is level, otherwise tap the container gently to level it. This also helps to bring any air bubbles to the surface.

THE PROJECTS

The amount of time we have available to express our creativity depends on our lifestyles and commitments – some people come home from work on Friday and are looking for something to keep them occupied for a couple of days, whereas others are trying to grab a few hours between the demands of home and children. Whatever your circumstances the projects in this book are designed to be made in several hours rather than days. Some may take an evening and others a little longer but as long as you have the materials to hand, none should take more than six to seven hours.

Many of the projects are designed to be used in the home, and most are ideal as gifts, though they are all so beautiful you may find yourself reluctant to give anything away.

Although many natural products are available all year round in craft stores, you may find that you are influenced by the seasons when deciding what to make. There are wonderful autumn and winter projects such as the Cone and Acorn Wreath (page 52), the Five-pines Box (page 48) or the Golden Nut Tree (page 74) and beautiful projects for the spring and summer such as the Bridal Keepsakes Box (page 44), Beach Memories Plaque (page 24) and the Sea-glass Candleholder (page 30).

For something a little different why not try making one of the projects that use crystal resin, plaster of paris or self-hardening clay as a base, such as the little Japanese Sushi Dishes (page 66), Miniature-shell Tiles (page 20) or the Fruit Coasters (page 90).

Indeed there are so many wonderful ideas in this book that it is likely that you will be crafting with natural materials for years to come.

MINIATURE-SHELL TILES

Anyone who has spent any amount of time on a beach has probably collected at least some of the tiny, perfectly formed shells that have miraculously remained uncrushed by the great forces of the waves. Beautiful though they are, it can be difficult to know what do with them when you get them home – until now.

These tiles are made from plaster of paris set in a bed of clay. You will also need a stiff material for the sides of your mould. Perspex (acrylic), suitable for picture framing, is ideal but you could use thin metal such as copper or aluminium, folding it in half before cutting to size if it is pliable enough. Tiles that will be placed close to a sink should be protected with several coats of matt varnish.

Instructions for making the delightful shell candles shown here are on page 33.

MINIATURE-SHELL TILES

YOU WILL NEED

- Small seashells of any variety you like
- Perspex (acrylic) or sheet metal
- Modelling clay
- Rolling pin
- Cutting mat or other non-absorbent surface on which to roll the clay
- Tracing paper, pencil and paper
- Glass-headed pin
- Scissors
- Plaster of paris
- Measuring jug
- Mixing bowl and old spoon
- Palette knife (optional)

Tip

To complete your project faster, cut additional strips of Perspex or metal so that you can make more than one tile at a time. However, measure out each quantity of plaster and water individually to ensure that each tile is the same thickness.

Cut four 2.5 x 10cm (1 x 4in) lengths of Perspex or sheet metal (see the tip, below left). Roll out the modelling clay until it is about 1cm (³⁄₈in) thick and approximately 12cm (4³⁄₄in) square. Lightly mark a 10cm (4in) square on the clay.

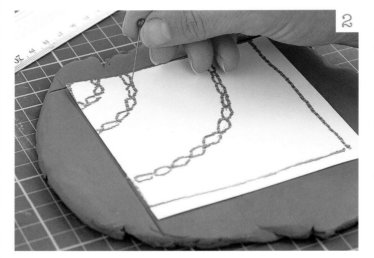

Trace the snail shell (page 94) or starfish design (page 95) from the template. Mark the direction of the shells and cut in four along the marked lines. Lay one of your new squares on the clay and prick along the shell lines with the pin.

Press two pieces of Perspex or metal into the clay along adjacent marked lines, making sure the corner is an exact right angle. Arrange the shells on the marked lines, as shown, following the direction indicated on the template. Note that the part of the shells embedded in the clay will lie on the top of the finished tile and the part that you see now will be hidden in the plaster. Press the shells gently so that they are half submerged in the clay.

Fit the remaining pieces of Perspex or metal so that they form an exact square with the other two pieces. Press a small ball of modelling clay over each corner of the Perspex to seal the join and prevent any plaster seeping out.

Measure out 60ml (4 tbsp) of water and pour into the mixing bowl. Pour 100g (3½oz) of plaster of paris into the water and mix gently to a thick cream. (Stirring rapidly creates too many air bubbles.) Add a little more water, if required.

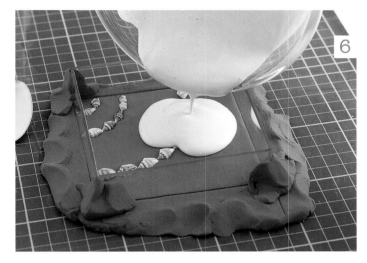

Pour the plaster mix into the tile mould and smooth the top with the back of a spoon, easing the mixture into the corners of the mould. Leave to dry for about an hour until completely set.

Once the plaster is dry, gently pull the Perspex strips out of the modelling clay. Ease the clay up at one side and lift off the work surface. You may need to slide a palette knife underneath to do this. Carefully peel the clay away from the tile and lay it on a non-absorbent surface to dry for a day or two. Make the other tiles in the same way.

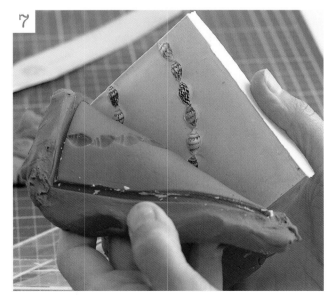

Try this
ORNATE TILES

For a more detailed look, completely fill the shell or starfish motif with small seashells or tiny pieces of sea glass. If you have any slightly damaged shells you can still use these, remembering that the side that is embedded in the clay will be on the top of the finished tile.

BEACH MEMORIES PLAQUE

One of the most idyllic ways to spend an afternoon on the beach is to go beach combing – wandering up and down the tide line searching for interesting bits and pieces such as seashells, driftwood, sea glass, crab shells, seaweed and any other attractive natural objects. A beach plaque is the ideal way to preserve the memories and mementos of such a wonderful time, and could be hung in a bathroom or a bedroom – anywhere you like to relax.

The frame is made from rough fence wood that has been waxed to create the weathered look of driftwood. Don't worry if you don't have enough findings to complete the plaque – you can buy starfish or unusual seashells from craft stores. You can even make a glass-pebble mat, as shown on page 29.

BEACH MEMORIES PLAQUE

YOU WILL NEED

- Found objects from the beach, including sand (see step 8), or suitable purchased items (see the tip opposite)

- 1m (1yd) of 12 x 25mm (½ x 1in) scraps of creosoted fencing wood

- 23cm (9in) square of 3mm (⅛in) hardboard for backing

- Paper and pen/pencil

- Saw

- Drill and drill bit

- Wood glue

- Hammer

- 3cm (1¼in) panel pins

- Heavy-duty staple gun and staples

- Wood stain the colour of the fencing wood

- Latex gloves

- Liming wax

- Jacobean wax

- Measuring jug

- Clean plastic container

- Plaster of paris

- Old spoon for mixing

- 25cm (10in) length of rope for hanging

Draw out a 21cm (8¼in) square on paper. Gather together your chosen items and sort out some small pieces, such as shells and starfish, to create a border at the top and bottom. Arrange the remaining pieces with larger items in the centre. Set the arrangement aside, making sure you keep everything in place.

Cut two 23.5cm (9¼in) lengths and two 21cm (8¼in) lengths of fencing wood. Drill two holes, 5mm (¼in) from the edges, at both ends of the longer pieces of wood.

Apply a little wood glue to the cut end of one of the shorter pieces. Position one of the longer pieces at right angles and hammer two panel pins into the drill holes to secure. Assemble the rest of the frame in the same way, remembering to glue each joint. Stain the cut ends of the wood to match the rest of the frame.

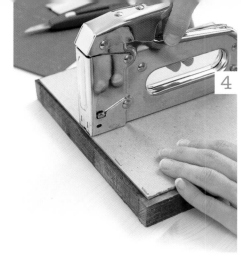

Place the frame face down on the work surface and position the square of hardboard on top. Staple in position with a heavy-duty staple gun. Keep the staples close to the edge to ensure that that they go into the frame.

Wearing latex gloves, rub liming wax over the entire frame and then wipe off any excess. The wax seals the frame as well as changing its colour. Apply a second coat of dark Jacobean wax to turn the wood frame an attractive shade of 'driftwood' grey.

Measure out 280ml (10 fl oz) of water in a clean plastic container. Gently pour in 400g (14oz) of plaster of paris on top. Stir slowly to create a thick, creamy mixture. (Stirring rapidly creates too many air bubbles.) Pour into your frame, making sure it goes into the corners and then tap the frame gently so that large air bubbles rise to the surface and can be pricked.

Working fairly quickly now, transfer the pieces of the border pattern from the paper (see step 1) onto the wet plaster. At this stage the plaster is still quite soft, so it is not necessary to press these fairly small pieces down.

Tip

If you never visit a beach, you can still make a plaque using seashells, sea glass, starfish and other items bought from a craft store. Sprinkle play sand over the wet plaster, and use natural sisal rope to hang the plaque.

BEACH MEMORIES PLAQUE

8 Transfer the larger pieces into the centre of the plaque, pressing gently to sink them into the plaster slightly. Position the remaining pieces as quickly as possible. To finish, sprinkle some beach sand over the entire surface of the plaster. Leave to dry for about an hour until completely set.

9 Use your 25cm (10in) piece of rope (either some found on the beach or natural sisal rope) to hang the picture. First open out the ends of the rope to create a flat surface, then turn the plaque over and staple it to the wood frame at the top edge, as shown.

Try this

GLASS-PEBBLE MAT

Use the same technique as given here to make a glass-pebble mat (see opposite) to protect your table from scorch marks from hot pots. First make a mould from strips of Perspex or metal (see Miniature-shell Tiles steps 3–4, pages 22–23) or find a suitable container that you can use instead. Pour in the plaster of paris mix and arrange the glass pebbles in simple patterns, such as circles, semi-circles and quarter circles. Leave for about an hour to set completely and then carefully remove the mould. Leave on a non-absorbent surface to dry out for several days. A piece of felt glued to the underside of each mat will prevent it from scratching a valuable table.

SEA-GLASS CANDLEHOLDER

There is nothing quite like a barbecue in summer, and with luck the evening will be warm enough to relax afterwards and enjoy a glorious sunset. As the light begins to fade, candles provide welcome additional light and add a romantic mood, made more glorious by the use of this colourful candleholder.

Although you can protect a candle from the whimsies of the breeze by placing it in a plain glass, the addition of sea-glass decorations adds colour and individuality. Or you could make the design your own by using small seashells or shingle to decorate the candleholder instead. If short of time you can combine gel wax with shells to make attractive quick-and-easy night-lights (see page 33).

SEA-GLASS CANDLEHOLDER

YOU WILL NEED

- Clear glass candleholder (see the tip on page 33)
- Selection of sea-glass chips
- Paper and pencil
- Tracing paper
- Scissors
- Masking tape
- Whiteboard marker or chinagraph pencil
- Towel
- Mosaic glue
- Mosaic grout
- Latex gloves
- Sponge
- Soft cloth

Measure the circumference of the glass and cut a strip of paper approximately 15cm (6in) deep and long enough to wrap around the candleholder. Wrap the paper around the glass and cut it exactly to size. Fold the paper in four and then unfold. Now trace the design from page 99 and trace one repeat in each quarter section. (See the tip opposite.)

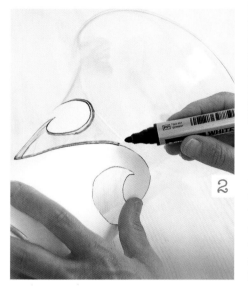

Cut along the curved pencil line and tape the template around the lamp. Draw around the curved edge of the template with a whiteboard marker or chinagraph and then remove the template.

Open out the template again and lay it on a flat surface. Arrange the pieces of sea glass on top with the darkest ones at the bottom. If possible, shade the pieces so that the tips of the waves fade to white.

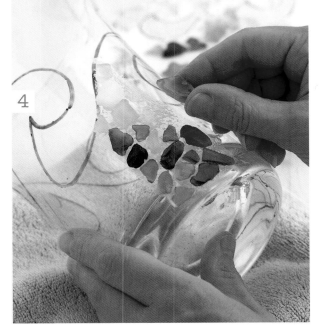

Nestle the candleholder on a folded towel to prevent it rolling around. Now spread mosaic glue on a small area at the bottom of the glass and begin to transfer the pieces of sea glass onto it. Work on sections of about 5cm (2in) at a time and leave each section to dry before turning the lamp and gluing on the next section. Leave the lamp to dry for at least 24 hours to ensure the glue has set thoroughly.

Tip

The template is designed to fit a candleholder with a 32cm (12$^1/_2$cm) circumference – each repeat is 8cm (3$^1/_8$in) wide. To fit a larger candleholder you could either enlarge the template or draw freehand to join up the gaps, keeping the design in the same style to fit around the lamp.

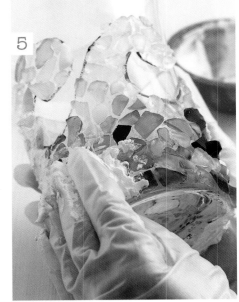

Mix sufficient grout powder with water to make a smooth paste. Wearing latex gloves, work it in between the pieces of glass by hand, taking care not to dislodge the larger ones. Remove most of the excess grout by wiping lightly with your fingers.

As the grout begins to set, wipe off any excess with a sponge. Rinse the sponge in a bucket of water frequently as you work, otherwise you will just keep reapplying the grout. Once completely dry, polish with a soft, dry cloth.

Try this SHELL NIGHT-LIGHTS

Pretty little shell night-lights can be made using the same techniques and gel wax, a clear gel that burns just like candle wax. Tie a length of candlewick to a small shell and drop it in the bottom of a glass. Partly fill the glass with larger shells, keeping the wick in the centre. Drape or tie the wick end to a pencil, balanced over the top of the glass. Melt the gel wax, following the manufacturer's instructions, and then pour over the shells. Allow to cool and then trim the wick to finish.

SUMMER FLOWERS CLOCK

Enjoy the colour and vibrancy of your summer garden all year round with this superb floral clock, which features a selection of pressed flowers and foliage. You can press fresh flowers and leaves remarkably quickly in the microwave (see Techniques, page 16) but if you can't find a good selection you can still make the clock, using pressed flowers from your local craft supplier.

The circular base for the clock is a ready-made blank, usually sold for use in pyrography, that can be stained and painted to whatever colour you like. The small clay tiles are so quick and easy to make with self-hardening clay that you can definitely complete your own floral clock in a weekend.

Any pressed flowers and pieces of left-over clay can be used to make a delightful greetings card (see pages 38–39).

SUMMER FLOWERS CLOCK

YOU WILL NEED

- Selection of pressed flowers and leaves

- 25cm (10in) plywood clock blank (or whatever size you like) with a set of hands and clock mechanism

- Tweezers

- Terracotta self-hardening clay

- Rolling pin

- Cutting mat (see the tip on page 38)

- Vegetable knife

- Pencil

- Scissors

- Compass

- Glass-headed pin

- Paintbrush

- Dark wood stain, such as chestnut

- Stone-coloured colourwash paint

- Two-way glue and silicone glue

- Clear polyurethane varnish

- Terracotta acrylic paint

1 Copy the template on pages 96–97 and make a second copy. Arrange flowers and leaves in the spaces around one of the templates to create a balanced arrangement of colours and shapes. Use tweezers to hold the small pieces. Set aside.

2 Roll out half a pack of terracotta clay on the reverse side of a cutting mat or similar moveable flat surface. Keep turning the mat to make the clay shape as round as possible. Stop when you can just fit the clock blank on the clay.

3 Mark the centre point of the clock through the hole and cut away the excess clay around the clock blank with your knife.

4 On your second paper template mark out from each line in pencil and then cut out the circle, saving the outside area. Lay this outside piece around the clay circle. Hold the vegetable knife between one of the marks on the paper and the centre point on the clay and press down to mark and cut the clay like a cake.

Open the compass to the radius of the inside circle on the template and lightly draw the inner circle on the clay. Cut along the marked line and carefully lift out. **5**

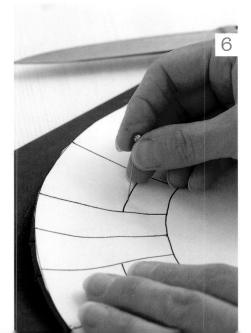

6 Lay the template over the clay, matching the lines, and pinprick to mark the dividing lines. Cut along these lines with the point of the vegetable knife. Leave the clay on the cutting mat and allow it to dry out overnight.

7 Wipe the clock blank with a dark wood stain and leave to dry for an hour or so. Paint a coat of colourwash over the stained wood to create a rustic finish and leave to dry.

SUMMER FLOWERS CLOCK

8 Working with one flower or leaf at a time, spread a thin layer of two-way glue on the reverse side and stick onto the corresponding clay tile. Continue until all the tiles are decorated.

9 Transfer the clay tiles onto the clock blank. The clay tiles shrink slightly as they dry, so you will need to space them evenly. Dot silicone glue on the back of each tile and stick onto the clock blank.

10 Glue four attractive leaves, such as Acer (maple) leaves, in the centre of the clock to mark the quarters. Paint the entire clock with two coats of polyurethane varnish and leave to dry. Now paint the clock hands to match the colour of the clay. Fit the clock mechanism into the hole in the centre of the clock, following the manufacturer's instructions, and press the hands in position to finish.

Tip

Do not try to lift the clay off the mat until it has dried. If you don't have a suitable mat, roll and mark the clay on the kitchen work surface in the evening and leave there to dry until the morning.

Try this GREETINGS CARDS

Don't waste leftover clay – it can be used to make your own greetings cards. Roll out the clay to make small, luggage-tag size tiles and make a hole at the top before leaving them to dry. To decorate, stick one or more flowers or leaves on each tile. Varnish the tiles and tie a loop of raffia through the hole. Decorate the cards with handmade paper and raffia or mesh ribbon and stick the tile in place with silicone adhesive.

WINTER LEAF TRAY

There is something particularly **beautiful** about skeleton leaves, with their **delicate** traceries of veins and their attached **memories** of childhood days spent rummaging about under the trees. But you don't have to go to any lengths to find these leaves because they can be bought in wonderful **colours** from your local craft shop. Complete the design with **handmade** mulberry paper, which can be bought at the same time.

To take advantage of the wonderful **transparency** of skeleton leaves, they have been overlapped to form a border on the rim, and turned into **sweeping** branches across the base using toning mulberry paper for the stems. Another idea is to embellish skeleton leaves with raffia and beads to decorate a **photo album** cover, as shown on page 43.

WINTER LEAF TRAY

YOU WILL NEED

- 5, 7.5 and 10cm (2, 3 and 4in) skeleton leaves in leaf green, sky blue, light navy, pale turquoise and mid turquoise

- Blue-grey mulberry paper

- 35 x 45cm (13$\frac{1}{2}$ x 17$\frac{1}{2}$in) blank wooden tray

- White emulsion paint

- Cream colourwash

- Paintbrush

- PVA (white) glue

- Glue brush

- Tracing paper and pencil

- Scissors and sharp craft knife

- Clear matt varnish or Mod Podge (see the tip, opposite)

Paint the tray with two coats of white emulsion and leave to dry overnight. Apply the cream colourwash over the top, brushing it in random directions to create a rough, rustic look. Leave to dry for several hours.

Fold a large skeleton leaf over the rim of the tray so that the point comes halfway down the outside of the tray. Trim the base off the leaf so that it fits flush into the join between the sides and the base. Brush some glue over the inside edge of the tray and over onto the outside and stick the leaf in place.

Work around the edge of the tray, trimming the leaves as before and overlapping them slightly so that the top rim of the tray is completely covered. Change the colours of the leaves fairly randomly to achieve a good colour balance. Stick the leaves straight over the handle holes at this stage.

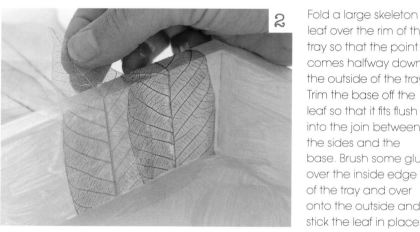

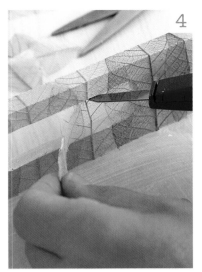

4 Tuck the leaves into each corner and trim along the fold lines before gluing. If there is any tray showing on the rim, cut a small piece of skeleton leaf to fit and glue in place. Once the glue has dried trim round the handle holes with a sharp craft knife.

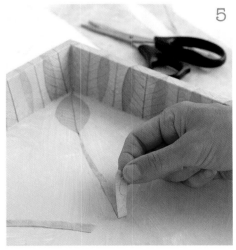

5 Trace the stem of the leaf template from page 98 four times onto blue-grey mulberry paper. Cut out just inside the lines. Stick a small leaf in each corner of the tray. Stick the stems in place so that the point of each one is at the bottom of the leaf and the base of each of the stems is towards the centre of the tray.

Tip

Mod Podge is a thick white liquid that looks like PVA (white) glue and is used mainly in découpage. It is ideal for sealing the leaves on the tray because it fills the gaps and dries clear. To make the tray very hard-wearing, apply several coats of Mod Podge (or varnish), leaving it to dry thoroughly between coats, until the leaves are completely sealed.

6 Using the template on page 98 as a guide, position another small leaf on either side of each stem and then two medium-sized leaves on each side. Depending on space, fill the remaining area at the bottom of each stem with one or two small leaves. Leave the glue to dry and then brush the entire tray with two coats of matt varnish or Mod Podge.

Try this

PHOTO ALBUM

This delightful little photo album is made using an album kit that comes complete with pre-cut card shapes and photo page inserts. (See Suppliers, page 102 for stockists.) Follow the manufacturer's simple instructions to cover the pre-cut card with pretty papers and make the album up ready to decorate. Then add your leaf decorations using the photograph, right, as your guide. Alternatively, buy a ready-made album and decorate it with handmade paper, natural raffia, skeleton leaves and gold beads in the same way. Use a clear-drying glue to attach the leaves and beads.

BRIDAL KEEPSAKES BOX

A bridal keepsakes box is a lovely gift to make for a friend who is getting married, and because roses are the symbol of love, these make the ideal decoration. The bride can use the box to keep memorabilia from the day, including photographs, greetings cards, telegrams and even cake decorations, or you could make one to store other personal items.

The box shown was decorated with dried rosebuds, which can be bought from craft shops. These could match the bride's bouquet or the bridesmaids' dresses. Alternatively, it would be a lovely idea to dry the actual roses from the bride's bouquet using silica gel (see Techniques, pages 14–15) and decorate the box with these. Use the same method to make a card, shown near right, or a rosebud ball (see page 47).

BRIDAL KEEPSAKES BOX

YOU WILL NEED

- 24cm (9¹/₂in) heart-shaped papier-mâché box

- Dried rosebuds: approximately 18 cream, 18 mottled pink, 22 dark pink and 42 deep red

- Cream-coloured rough handmade paper large enough to cover the box and lid

- White acrylic or emulsion paint

- Cream colourwash, preferably in the same shade as the paper

- Paintbrush

- PVA (white) glue

- Scissors

- Pencil and paper

- Clear silicone adhesive

- 1m (1¹/₄yd) of 2cm (⁷/₈in) wire-edged ribbon

Tip

Don't be tempted to use scissors to cut the flaps of paper around the top and bottom of the box because this will not be as neat as tearing the glued paper. When handmade paper is damp it tears more easily and leaves a ragged edge that blends into the paper it overlaps. When it dries the paper appears to be seamless.

Paint the outside of the papier-mâché box with two coats of white paint and leave to dry thoroughly. (This prevents the box colour showing through the paper). Paint the inside of the lid and the box with a coat of cream colourwash and leave to dry.

Dilute glue with an equal amount of water. Cut a piece of handmade paper slightly deeper than the box base and long enough to cover half of it. Brush the reverse of the paper with the diluted glue and then the side of the box. Press the paper onto the side of the box and turn the top edge to the inside. Tear the paper around the bottom edge every so often and paste onto the base of the box (see the tip below left). Repeat on the other half and then cover the base with a heart-shaped piece of paper.

Now cover the lid, taking the paper up the sides and tucking the edges inside. Paste the paper and lid as before, tearing the damp paper where necessary to overlap and avoid folds. Leave to dry. Trace the template on page 99 and cut out the heart shapes. Trace the heart shapes onto the box lid.

4 Choose about 18 small cream rosebuds and trim the stem off each bud where it begins to swell out, leaving the sepals in place if possible. Dab a little silicone adhesive on the bottom of each bud and stick to the centre heart on the box lid, filling it completely.

5 Trimming the stems off as before, stick a row of mottled pink roses around the cream roses and then stick a row of dark pink roses around these. Use the pencil lines as a guide. Finish with a row of deep red roses.

7 Take the ribbon and, beginning with the middle of the ribbon at the bottom point of the lid, wrap it around the lid rim. Tie the ribbon in a bow at the top and stick in place with silicone adhesive.

6 Complete the mosaic by sticking about eight red roses on each side to fill out the heart shape. Break off some large sepals from some spare rosebuds and stick carefully under the outside rosebuds to finish the design.

Try this ROSEBUD BALL

Make a rosebud ball as a gift for the bride as she leaves the church or for a bridesmaid to carry instead of a bouquet. All you need is a foam ball, some ribbon and dried rosebuds. First tie a length of ribbon around a dry-foam ball and trim the ends. Tie a second length around the ball to divide it in four, leaving long ends to hang. Fill the four areas of exposed foam with rosebuds, gluing them in place with silicone glue. Arrange the ribbon ends into a loop so that it can be hung from the wrist.

FIVE-PINES BOX

The wonderful **woody** smell of pine cones is definitely peculiar to winter and heralds log fires, hot drinks and the onset of **Christmas**. The cones look wonderful in the home arranged on shelves, hung from the ceiling by ribbons or combined with candles, but it is nice if you can do something more permanent with them.

The box on the far right combines five **varieties** of cone in different colours to create the patterns, colours and **textures**. You may be lucky enough to pick these up for nothing in parks or woods, but if not you can always buy some different varieties from craft shops and floral suppliers (and see the tip on page 51). For the sides you will need fine twigs of **willow** or thin bark from a eucalyptus tree.

If you would like to try an alternative design, such as the lid near right, turn to page 51 for further **ideas**.

FIVE-PINES BOX

YOU WILL NEED

- Five varieties of pine cones or fir cones in different colours such as Douglas fir (Oregon fir), ponderosa, red pine, austrica, sand pine, sugar pine and so on (or see the tip, opposite)

- Fine willow branches or similar

- 20cm (8in) diameter papier-mâché box

- Secateurs

- Saw (optional)

- Craft knife

- Scissors

- Craft glue, such as PVA (white) glue, which is clear drying

- hot-glue gun and glue sticks or silicone adhesive

- Glue brush

- Pencil

Start by removing the scales from your pine cones. To do this first cut off the base of the cone using secateurs or a saw. Then cut across the base of each scale individually using secateurs or a craft knife.

For the rim of the lid you will need roughly 50 of the scales from a pine cone such as sand pine. Spread craft glue over a section of the lid rim. Press the pine cone scales into the glue so that the end of each one is flush with the top of the lid. Once the rim is covered in scales allow the glue to dry completely and then trim the rough edges of the scales flush with the bottom of the lid.

Cut off the base of several dark pine cones and cut off approximately 45 scales. If necessary, trim the end off each one so that it will lie flat. Spread glue around the edge of the box lid and arrange the scales side by side. You can trim the sides of the scales so that they fit flush together.

Repeat the process with a reddish cone such as sand pine or austrica, and then create a third ring with larger, darker scales such as those from ponderosa. Take care when cutting ponderosa scales because they have a sharp spike on the end.

To create an attractive centrepiece, opt for a change of colour and texture. Use something like Douglas (Oregon) fir. As before, carefully trim off the base of the cone, then cut off approximately 20 scales. Stick these down in two rows to cover the rough edges of the ponderosa pine.

5

For the centre pine cone 'flower' cut the base off an austrica or sand pine cone, or something similar. You can use a pair of strong secateurs or a saw to do this. Glue the 'flower' in the centre of the lid using a glue gun or silicone adhesive.

6

Tip

Don't worry if you can't find all the varieties of cones used for the box. Just get together what you can and see how you can arrange them into a pattern. If you don't have enough colour variation, you can dye batches of cone scales with wood dye or food colouring before beginning to assemble them.

7

Put the lid on the box base and mark where the rim finishes with a light pencil line. Using the thin tops of the willow branches, cut lengths to fit between the marked line and the base of the box. Working on a small area at a time, spread glue over the box up to the line and stick on the cut willow pieces, side by side. Leave to dry.

Try this EMBELLISHED BOX LID

If you are really short of pine-cone varieties or want to try something different, consider covering just the centre of the box lid in a shape such as a heart or with somebody's initials. Use the shaped tips of large pine cone scales for this. And if you can't get hold of willow or other suitable twigs for the sides, try bark. The box shown right and on pages 48–49 has its sides covered in strips of eucalyptus bark. To flatten bark, dampen it, roll it inside out and leave to dry.

CONE AND ACORN WREATH

Decking out the home with baubles, tinsel and greenery for Christmas lifts our spirits and turns our thoughts towards our families. Even before family and friends enter your house, a wreath on the front door is there to welcome them. It is just a shame that these gorgeous decorations are hung for such a short time.

This wreath has been designed without sparkle or glitter so that it can be hung in your home for the whole of the autumn and winter. The beautiful reindeer moss is available in a range of bright colours from your local craft shop so you could even co-ordinate it with your décor.

CONE AND ACORN WREATH

YOU WILL NEED

- 25cm (10in) polystyrene or dry-foam wreath
- Acorns
- Douglas fir cones (Oregon fir) or other medium to large cones
- Two varieties of small pine cones such as hemlock spruce and black spruce
- Measuring tape
- Pencil and paper
- WD40 or other light oil
- Silicone adhesive (or see the tip, opposite)
- Secateurs
- Green reindeer moss
- Red paper ribbon for hanging the wreath

Mark the foam wreath into quarters with a pencil line. Cut a strip of paper to fit between the marks on the inside and another for the outside of the wreath and fold each strip of paper in half and half again. Unfold and hold the paper against the wreath to mark each quarter section at the folds. Work all round on each side of the wreath. Join opposite marks with a pencil line. Draw a line about 1cm (½in) away from each side of one of the lines for the ribbon.

Wipe the acorns with a little WD 40 or other light oil to give them a shine. Stick an acorn to the inside of the wreath on the second line from the ribbon so that it is resting on your work surface. Stick more acorns along the line until the last one rests on the work surface on the other side. Miss three lines and stick on another row of acorns. Repeat until there are four rows.

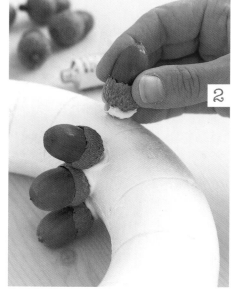

Cut the base off several large (Douglas fir) cones using secateurs and trim the scales. You will need approximately 45, divided into three groups of 15. Count four lines from the ribbon position and, beginning on the outside of the wreath, stick on the scales so that they overlap. Miss three lines and stick on another row of scales. Repeat until there are three rows of scales.

Spread a narrow band of silicone adhesive around the wreath on one of the remaining lines. Trim the stem off approximately nine 2cm (¾in) hemlock cones. Stick them side-by-side into the silicone adhesive so that the last cone at each end is resting on the work surface. Miss three lines and then stick on another row of hemlock cones. Repeat until there are four lines of cones.

Glue a row of your other variety of small cones (black spruce) along each of the remaining marked lines. As before, the last cones on each side should be flush with the work surface.

Prepare the reindeer moss by removing any pine needles or other foreign matter. Remove any dark or withered moss. Spread a thin layer of silicone adhesive in the area between the first line of cones and acorns. Now press the moss into the adhesive to cover the foam completely. Repeat around the wreath.

Stick moss on each side of the ribbon area and then tie a ribbon around the wreath in the gap. Hang on a door or wall or stand the wreath on a shelf.

Tip

If you have a dry-foam wreath you can use a hot-glue gun to stick the cones and moss in position. The hot glue is unsuitable for a polystyrene wreath because it melts the surface.

RUSTIC WILLOW TROUGH

Willow is a beautiful material that is traditionally harvested in winter when the sap is down. Basket weavers use it fresh, while it is still pliable, but it is also available dried for use in the home, where it can be gathered into a bundle with sea grass or raffia as a design accent. Fresh willow can be stripped of its bark easily to leave beautiful white branches but older wood requires soaking for several hours in boiling water when the tannin from the bark gives it the traditional buff colour often seen in basketry.

This trough takes advantage of the colour contrast between stripped and unstripped willow to make its striking chequered design. Willow cut into strips or mini logs can be combined with other natural products to make the picture frames on pages 60–61.

RUSTIC WILLOW TROUGH

YOU WILL NEED

- Willow bundle
- 35 x 12 x 12cm (13³/₄ x 5 x 5in) blank plant trough
- Serrated knife
- Vegetable knife
- Dark wood stain similar to the colour of the willow bark
- Latex gloves
- Polyurethane varnish
- Paintbrush
- Pencil
- Ruler
- Secateurs
- Wood glue
- Glue brush
- Masking tape

Cut about a dozen lengths of willow that will fit into the kitchen sink and scrape down each piece lightly with a serrated knife to break the dark bark. Cover the willow with very hot water and leave to soak for several hours. Using a vegetable knife, gently scrape the dark bark and the lighter inner skin off without damaging the wood. Leave to dry overnight.

Stain the blank planter with dark wood stain. To make it waterproof on the inside and to prevent damage from water spillage, paint with two coats of polyurethane varnish and allow it to dry.

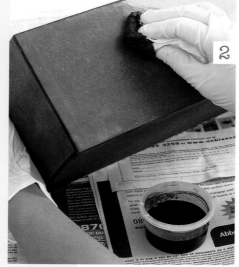

Tip

Stripped willow bundles are available – if you find one then you can skip step 1 and go straight to step 2.

Measure halfway down the planter and draw a line all the way round as a guideline for the willow decoration. Using a pair of secateurs cut the willow sticks into 6cm (2¹/₂in) lengths. You will need approximately 125 pieces in both dark and stripped willow in a variety of thicknesses to cover this size of planter.

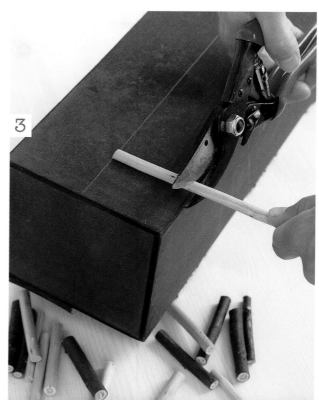

Spread wood glue over one end surface of the planter. Stick pieces of stripped willow horizontally up as far as the line to cover one quarter. Stick pieces of dark willow vertically to the edge of the stripped willow. Complete the other half of the panel to finish the pattern.

4

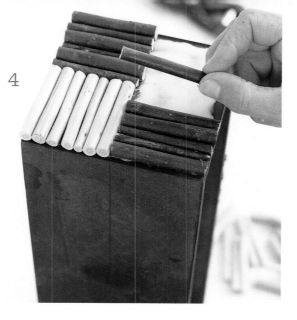

5

Spread wood glue over a 6cm (2½in) strip on the front of the planter. Continuing the chequered pattern, stick horizontal pieces of stripped willow in the top-left corner so that the pieces jut out over the end of the planter, level with the willow on the end panel.

6

Stick the first piece of dark willow next to the stripped willow of the end panel and then compete the chequered pattern as before. Check that the willow will jut out at the other end to cover the ends of the willow on the side panel and adjust the pattern as necessary before the glue dries completely.

7

Once the pattern is finished on all four sides, cut two pieces of willow to fit across the top-front edge of the planter. Stick in place with wood glue. Stick two more pieces on the back edge and then cut pieces to fit in between for the side edges to complete the planter. Secure the wood trim with masking tape until the glue dries.

Try this MINI-LOG PICTURE FRAMES

You can decorate plain picture frames using exactly the same technique as for the trough (pages 58–59) or try a mini-log frame as explained here. Start with a flat wooden frame and press a specimen leaf to mount in it.

YOU WILL NEED

- Willow bundle or other wood (see step 2)
- Specimen leaf
- Wooden frame
- Dark wood stain
- Secateurs
- Wood glue
- Glue brush
- Paper

Tip

Cut the mini logs for the picture frames while the wood is still fresh and then leave to dry out before making the frame. Thicker branches from garden plants such as Virginia Creeper are ideal for making the logs.

Stain a flat wooden frame with a dark wood stain to match the colour of the dark willow. Using secateurs, cut pieces of willow to fit around the aperture of the frame and stick in place with wood glue. Cut lengths of willow to fit diagonally across the corners of the frame, trimming the ends at an angle so that they are level with the frame edge; stick in place.

Choose several different thicknesses of willow or other wood such as birch or dogwood and cut mini logs about 5–12mm (¼–½in) long with the secateurs.

Glue the thickest mini logs in the areas between the twigs and fill in the gaps with very thin twigs. It is easiest to dab glue onto the end of a twig, fit it into a small gap and then trim to length with the secateurs.

Press a leaf in the microwave (see Techniques, page 16) and stick onto a piece of off-white paper. Mount inside the frame to finish.

DECORATIVE HOUSE PLAQUE

Dried beans and pulses make **wonderful** mosaic decorations because they keep well for such a long time and come in lovely **natural** shades – soft reds, mottled greens, warm browns and yellows. Most people have some in the back of the store cupboard but otherwise they are **inexpensive** to buy in your local health-food store or supermarket and you might even enjoy adding them to your cooking too!

Choose **beans** that are not cracked or chipped in any way and paint the finished plaque with several coats of matt varnish to protect it from the elements. This way it should stand **proudly** outside your house for several years.

This technique can easily be adapted for other items, such as **storage jars** (see page 65.)

DECORATIVE HOUSE PLAQUE

YOU WILL NEED

- Brown and orange lentils, black beans, yellow split peas and flageolet beans

- 25cm (10in) blank oval wooden plaque

- Flush fittings or silicone adhesive for hanging the plaque

- Latex gloves

- Antique pine stain

- Tracing paper

- Paper and pencil

- Scissors

- Craft knife to cut the stencil

- PVA (white) glue (see the tip, below)

- Glue brush

- Tweezers

- Clear varnish

- Paintbrush

Tip

It is important that you use a clear-drying adhesive to stick the beans and pulses in place or your lovely plaque will be ruined by visible blobs of dried glue. Before you begin the project it is a good idea to test the technique first to make sure that everything goes as planned.

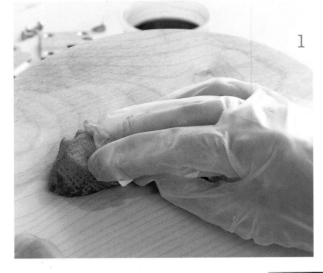

1 Wearing latex gloves, stain both sides of the plaque with antique pine stain and leave to dry. If you plan to have a removable plaque, fit flush fastenings to the reverse side at this stage.

2 Trace the number(s) you require onto paper from the templates on page 100 and cut out just inside the lines to create your own stencil. Position the stencil in the centre of the plaque and draw lightly around the outline to mark the numbers.

3 Dab glue inside the lines and cover with brown lentils, using tweezers to help place them. Use single and double rows of lentils to make the numbers look more interesting.

4 Dab a little glue around the outside edge of the plaque and stick on a few orange lentils, side by side. Create a second row with alternate orange and brown lentils and finish the pattern with a row of orange lentils. Continue around the edge in the same way, repeating the three rows to complete the border.

5 Referring to the template on page 101, arrange the black beans and yellow split peas on the plaque to make the large flowers. Draw faint pencil lines between them to mark the position of the brown lentil lines. Stick the beans and split peas in position and then stick brown lentils along the pencil lines.

6 Stick a yellow split pea on the plaque, as marked on the template, for each of the small flowers and stick a ring of orange lentils around each one for the petals.

Try this
STORAGE JARS

You can experiment with dried beans and pulses, or even shells, on other surfaces. One idea is to use these to decorate storage jars. Cut a section from a dry-foam ball and stick it to the lid. Then glue beans and pulses onto the foam to cover it completely. Create a decorative motif on the front of the jar to finish.

7 Finally, stick the flageolet bean 'leaves' in position along the wavy brown lentil lines. Leave the glue to dry for 24 hours. Paint the entire plaque with two coats of clear varnish to finish. Hang using the flush fittings or stick in place with silicone adhesive.

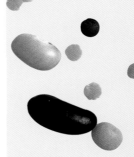

JAPANESE SUSHI DISHES

The Japanese knack of creating elegance from simplicity has led to a spread of Japanese designs around the world, and now that more and more people are sampling the cuisine of other nations, flat dishes like these are a familiar sight everywhere.

Inspired by beautiful Japanese porcelain bowls with their translucent rice patterns, these dishes use black and sushi rice to mark out the designs. They feature the traditional Kanji characters for 'man', 'woman' and 'child', so you can create one for all the members of the family, and if they aren't fond of sushi, they can still use their dishes for their favourite nibbles. Alternatively, use this idea to make a plaque for a bamboo pot (see page 69).

JAPANESE SUSHI DISHES

YOU WILL NEED

- Self-hardening clay
- Black Emperor rice
- Sushi or pudding rice
- Cutting mat
- Rolling pin
- Large kitchen knife
- Paper and pencil
- Scissors
- Glass-headed pin
- Tweezers
- Shellac
- Paintbrush
- Methylated spirits

Tip

Wrap all spare clay
in a damp cloth and put it
back in the polythene bag it
came in to prevent
it drying out.

Roll out some clay on the cutting mat to about 3 or 4mm (⅛in) thick and mark out a rectangle approximately 10 x 12cm (4 x 4¾in) with a kitchen knife. Trace or photocopy one of the Japanese character templates from pages 94–95. Cut out the character and position on the clay on the left-hand side. Use the glass-headed pin to prick lightly around the edge of the design to transfer it.

Using tweezers, arrange the grains of black rice to fill the area inside the pinpricks. Keep the rice running lengthways along the design and change from two to three grains where the line widens sufficiently. Press gently with your fingers to sink the rice slightly into the clay.

Arrange five grains of sushi rice into a little flower and position on the right-hand side of the Japanese motif. Make three or four flowers to complete the design. Press in gently with your fingers and then roll over the whole design with a rolling pin to sink the rice into the clay.

Trim the clay rectangle to size – it will have been distorted slightly as you rolled the rice in. Roll out a piece of clay about 5mm (¼in) thick. Cut two 1 x 6cm (½ x 2¼in) strips to fit on the base for feet. Lay them upside down on the cutting mat and dampen with water. Lift the clay dish and position centrally on the clay strips. Press gently to stick.

4

5

To shape the dish, turn up the edges at each side. Bend the front and back edges of the dish in a gentle curve and leave to dry. Check that the base of the dish stays flat and doesn't sink as it dries. Make further dishes in the same way.

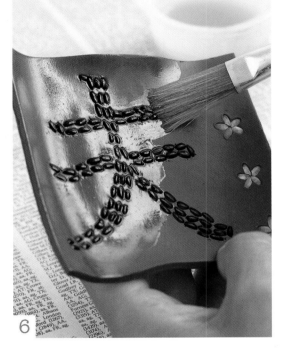

6

Once the clay dish has dried, paint it with two coats of shellac, leaving this to dry between coats. Leave the brush sitting in methylated spirits between coats (see the tip, above right). When you have finished, clean the shellac out of the brush with more methylated spirits.

Tip

Shellac is a traditional and very durable varnish made from insect resin. It is extremely difficult to remove from a brush and people who use it a lot, such as furniture restorers, often just keep the same brush soaking in methylated spirits between uses. To clean the brush it helps to soak it for a little while in methylated spirits before washing in hot soapy water. Do not use a treasured brush to apply shellac.

Try this

ORIENTAL MOTIF PLAQUE

This technique is so much fun and so easy to do that you'll probably want to use it more than once. Try making a plaque or a picture in the same way. Roll out a small piece of clay as in step 1, and then decorate it however you like in rice motifs. For a plaque, pierce small holes in each corner with a bamboo skewer. Lift the still-soft clay and lay it over a bamboo pot so that it dries in a curved shape. Once dry the plaque can be varnished with shellac and tied onto the pot with raffia.

EGGSHELL MOSAIC

Believe it or not, the mosaic **patterns** on these elegant accessories are made from the shells of the ordinary eggs you eat for breakfast. This delightful technique is really mosaic in **miniature** and is surprisingly **easy** to do.

It doesn't matter what colour of eggs you buy, as it is the white inside of the eggshell that becomes the top surface of the mosaic, but it is better to buy large eggs so that you can use the sides, which are less curved, for the mosaic. You can apply the eggshell mosaic to almost any flat surface, so you can add to your set by **decorating** the back of a hairbrush or perfume bottle. Step-by-step instructions are given to mosaic the box.

Instructions for how to make the pretty **photo frame** are given on page 73.

EGGSHELL MOSAIC

YOU WILL NEED

- 10cm (4in) square pine box
- Two large hen's eggs
- Tin embossing sheet
- Craft scissors
- Neoprene sheet or pad of paper
- Embossing tool (see the tip below)
- Pencil and ruler
- PVA (white) and mosaic glue
- Large darning needle or similar tool
- Black watercolour paint
- Artist's paintbrush
- Liming wax
- Kitchen towel
- Clean cloth
- Mosaic grout (ordinary grout is too coarse)
- Latex gloves
- Grout sponge
- Acrylic varnish

Tip

An embossing tool is the proper tool for drawing into the tin, but if you don't have one you can use a worn-out ballpoint pen instead. Make sure it is clean and completely out of ink before you begin. Alternatively you could use a cocktail stick or similar.

Wash out the shells of two large eggs and boil them in a pot of water for a few minutes. Once cool enough peel the membrane away from the inside of the shell. The boiling process sterilizes the shells and makes it easy to remove the membrane.

Cut a 3cm (1¼in) square of tin sheet. Lay the square on a neoprene mat or pad of newspaper and, using the embossing tool, draw a line around the edge as shown on the template on page 94. Draw the centre of the flower and then the petals. Fill the centre of the flower and the background with dots, as shown.

Mark a line 5mm (¼in) in from the edge of the box. Measure in 3cm (1¼in) from the line on each side to mark the position of the tin square in the centre of the box. Glue the square in place.

Mix some mosaic glue with a little water so that it takes longer to dry and apply to part of the box lid. Break off a piece of eggshell and lay it in the glue. Press with your finger to break it into small pieces then use a large darning needle to manoeuvre the bits so that there is a slight gap between each. Continue in this way up to the marked pencil line. Complete the eggshell mosaic and leave to dry a little.

Mix some black paint with water to create a wash and paint the eggshell for a mottled look. Leave to dry. Rub liming wax over the surface of the box, keeping the wax clear of the eggshell mosaic. Wipe off the excess with kitchen towel and buff to a shine with a cloth once it has dried.

Mix 30ml (2 tbsp) of mosaic grout powder with a little water to make a paste like double cream. Spoon some onto the mosaic and smooth between the gaps with your finger. Wipe off the excess. Leave to dry slightly and then gently wipe with a fine sponge to remove any remaining grout from the surface. Do not rub too hard or you will remove the paint. Once the grout has dried completely (30–40 minutes), buff lightly with kitchen towel. Brush the mosaic with acrylic varnish to finish.

Try this
EGGSHELL PHOTO FRAME

To make this pretty coordinating photo frame, take an ordinary wooden frame. Make and attach embossed tin motifs to each corner and the centre of each long edge. Then complete in the same way as the box, covering the remaining surface with eggshell.

GOLDEN NUT TREE

For many of us nuts are a Christmas essential, as much of a tradition as tinsel, fairy lights and Christmas trees. Part of that tradition is to buy them still in their shells and then sit by the fire in the evenings cracking into such favourites as brazils and almonds.

If you have some leftover from last year or ones you simply can't break into, don't throw them away – make them into a nut tree. The wonderfully different shapes and textures of the whole nuts make them ideal. Gilding wax and gold leaf add a festive feel and small pieces of pecan nut shells can be used to make a pretty Christmas motif for the front of the pot to add the finishing touch.

Compliment the look and display your lighting in the same style – see page 77.

GOLDEN NUT TREE

YOU WILL NEED

- Tall 12 cm (4³/₄in) diameter terracotta pot

- Mixed selection of nuts (walnuts, hazelnuts, brazil nuts, pecans and almonds) plus dried lychees (litchis), alder cones and open beechnuts, if possible

- Natural sponge

- Brick-red acrylic paint

- Two-way glue or leaf metal size

- Sheets of imitation gold leaf

- Stiff brush, such as a stencil brush

- Pencil and paper

- Scissors

- Mosaic glue

- Pebbles for weight

- Plaster of paris

- Two bamboo skewers

- 9cm (3¹/₂in) dry-foam cone

- Gilding wax

- Latex gloves

- Kitchen towel

- Hot-glue gun and glue sticks

Tip

To give the gilded pot an aged look, as shown in the photograph, overlap some edges but leave slight gaps in between some of the pieces so that the red paint shows through. You can also rub the gold leaf gently with fine sandpaper to distress it.

Sponge brick-red acrylic paint over the outside of the terracotta pot and leave to dry. Spread a thin layer of two-way glue over half the pot and leave to go clear. Meanwhile cut several sheets of gold leaf into eight rectangles. Lift the pieces one at a time; lay onto the glued area and press down. (See the tip, below left.)

Cover the whole pot in the same way then brush off the excess gold leaf with a stiff brush. Draw a star on white paper and cut out to make a stencil. Place the stencil on the front of the pot and draw around the star with pencil to transfer it.

Crack open a couple of pecan nuts. Remove the nuts and break the shell into pieces. Spread a little mosaic glue on one section of the star and begin to fit the shell pieces. If necessary, cut the shell with scissors to make the points of the star. Continue until the star is covered with shell mosaic and leave to dry.

Half fill the terracotta pot with pebbles to weigh it down. Mix enough plaster of paris in the proportion 10 parts of plaster to 6 parts of water to fill the rest of the pot and fill to the brim. Stick two bamboo skewers into the plaster. Leave the plaster until it begins to set. At this point, push the dry-foam cone onto the bamboo skewers. If the skewers stick out of the cone, trim off the ends with scissors.

4

6

Heat the glue gun and insert a glue stick. Spread a small amount of glue on the back of a nut and stick at the base of the cone. Work around the base, adding different nuts to cover it.

5

Wearing latex gloves, apply a small quantity of gilding wax to each nut. Rub the nuts between your fingers to spread the wax evenly over the surface. Wipe off any excess with a piece of kitchen towel and leave to dry off slightly.

Try this
FESTIVE CANDLES

If you are short of time, make a simple Christmas decoration using the decorated pot and a few gilded nuts. Simply set a 5cm (2in) wide pillar candle into the plaster of paris just before it sets. Use the glue gun to stick gilded nuts around the base of the candle to cover the plaster, then fill in any gaps with beech nuts and alder cones. As with any candle decoration, take care not to leave it unattended when lit.

7

Work up the cone, gluing different types of nut over the surface. Occasionally add a gilded lychee (litchi) if you have some and fill the small gaps with alder cones and open beechnuts. As you get to the top, use smaller nuts and push them into the foam to create an attractive pointed shape.

AROMATIC SPICE SPHERES

The wonderful shapes and colours of dried spices are as intriguing as their delicious and sometimes mysterious aromas, so even if you don't intend to cook with them you can still use them in the home for a display.

A spice sphere is quick to make and much easier than it looks. Use pretty spices such as whole cloves, star anise and cardamom from your store cupboard and look for interesting dried products in pot pourri mixes or from floral suppliers. Chinese supermarkets often have unusual dried products such as radish root, lemon grass and chillies that you could use. Aim to offset the pale natural colours with dark brown seed heads or cloves, and add a touch of colour with rich green cardamom pods and gorgeous red bora berries.

Use a similar idea to decorate church or pillar candles (see page 83.)

AROMATIC SPICE SPHERES

YOU WILL NEED

- Two 12cm (4¾in) dry-foam balls

- Map pins

- Measuring tape

- Hot-glue gun and glue sticks

- A selection of dried exotic produce:
  For the medallion ball
  puspa pods, durian seed heads, red bora berries, dried lemon grass and star anise seeds
  For the striped ball
  puspa pods, red bora berries, whole cloves, dried parsnip root and cardamon pods

Tip

A hot-glue gun makes it easy to stick the spices to the ball, but the appearance can be ruined by fine threads of glue. To prevent this happening, wipe the tip of the glue gun against the dry-foam ball before lifting it off.

MAKING THE MEDALLION BALL

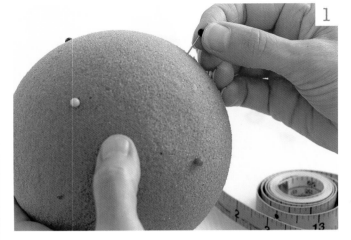

1 Stick a map pin into one of the dry-foam balls and then stick in another 7cm (2¾in) away. Stick in the third equidistant from the other two to form a triangle. Continue adding pins with approximately 7cm (2¾in) gaps in between until the ball is covered with equally spaced pins.

2 Heat the hot-glue gun and insert a glue stick. Lift out the map pins one at a time and apply a dot of hot glue to the surface. Stick a puspa pod in place of each map pin, or a different spice of your choice.

3 Apply a ring of glue around one of the puspa pods and stick brown durian seed heads in place. Repeat this process with the red bora berries. Repeat around all the puspa pods.

4 Sort through the dried lemon grass to find all the little tubes and put the rest to one side. Depending on the gaps between the decorative circles, stick one or two rings of lemon grass around each motif.

Try this
TOPIARY TREE

Make a topiary tree by fitting the ball onto a dowel and setting the dowel into a pretty terracotta pot.

5 There should be a small triangle left in the middle of each group of three decorative circles. Apply a little glue and stick three star anise seeds in the middle. Fill any gaps in the ball with pieces of lemon grass.

SPICE SPHERES

MAKING THE STRIPED BALL

1 Space puspa pods approximately every 6cm (2³/₈in) around the circumference of the dry-foam ball. Then stick a group of six bora berries in between each puspa pod and add another bora berry to the centre of every puspa pod.

2 Fill the gaps in the band with cloves. You do not need to glue these – simply push them into the foam. For the remaining rows apply slices of dried parsnip root and a row of cardamom pods stuck on diagonally.

Tip

When making the striped sphere, score the dry-foam ball with a knife to mark the outside lines of the wider bands. This helps you keep the lines straight.

Try this

FRAGRANT CANDLES

Use spices such as whole cloves and cinnamon sticks to make some sweet-smelling candles. Simply glue the cloves and cinnamon sticks onto the outside of wide church or pillar candles using clear-drying ultra-strong glue. Remember never to leave a candle unattended.

ORIENTAL LAMP BASE

Bamboo has found its way into many gardens around the world, but it has held onto its exotic origins and the sight of it conjures up images of all things Oriental. Its distinctive stems are ideal for printing into clay, and here this has been combined with gilding to give this lamp base an exotic note.

The small clay tiles decorated with a border of imitation gold leaf are suitable for decorating any flat surface – you could cover a box lid or even a small tabletop. An alternative idea is to make a relief image of the imprint. Try pressing bamboo leaves into clay to make a large tile in plaster of paris. Frame this with a mosaic of pressed bamboo leaves (see pages 88-89).

ORIENTAL LAMP BASE

YOU WILL NEED

- Plain 15 x 15 x 20cm (6 x 6 x 8in) lamp base (any colour)

- White self-hardening clay

- Rolling pin

- Cutting mat

- Kitchen knife

- Pieces of bamboo

- Two-way glue or gold size

- Sheets of imitation gold leaf

- Stencil brush or other stiff brush

- Shellac

- Paintbrush

- Methylated spirits

- Non-stick paper such as silicone or Bakewell

- Deep green acrylic paint

- Black patinating wax

- Soft cloth

- White spirit

- Kitchen towel

Tip

A cutting mat helps you cut the clay tiles to the exact size required. If you don't have one, cut a square of card as a template, lay it over each bamboo-printed clay square and trim to size.

Cut a piece of clay from the block and begin to roll it out on a cutting mat. It is easier to roll the clay if you keep lifting it after each sweep of the rolling pin and lay it down with a quarter turn every time. Roll out the clay to 5mm ($\frac{1}{4}$in). Cut a 6cm ($2\frac{1}{4}$in) strip and mark into 6cm ($2\frac{1}{4}$in) sections.

Press a piece of bamboo into the clay between the first two marks and roll gently from side to side. Some pieces of bamboo make more interesting marks, so it is a good idea to experiment on spare clay before you start. Change to a different width of bamboo and press into the next section. Vary where the bamboo imprint is in relation to the square.

Cut the strips into squares and then trim them to exactly 5cm (2in), using the lines on the cutting mat as a guide (or see the tip, left). Make 15 tiles for each side of the lamp base. Lay the tiles on a flat surface to dry. You can cover the tiles with a piece of board to keep them flat as they dry but this slows down the drying process.

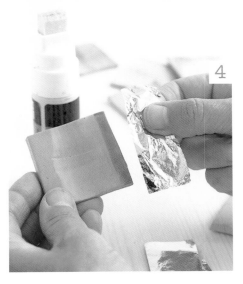

4 Spread a band of two-way glue or gold size down one side of a tile, adding a little on the edge of the tile too. Leave the glue to get tacky. With two-way glue this will take a minute or two; gold size takes about 15 minutes. Apply glue to several tiles at time, varying the width and position of the glue on each tile. Cut the gold leaf into strips that will fit over the glued area.

5 Lift a piece of gold leaf onto a tile to cover the glued area and press gently to stick it in place. Gild several tiles a time and then brush off the excess with a stiff (stencil) brush.

6 Paint each square with shellac and leave to dry on a piece of non-stick paper. Leave the brush to soak in methylated spirits for a little while and then rinse in hot, soapy water.

Tip

Collect the scraps of imitation gold leaf because these can be used to gild other objects. Simply use a stencil brush to pick up and tamp down the scraps onto the size. Once dry, brush off the excess. Use a wooden or metal container to collect the scraps because plastic attracts too much static.

7 Paint the lamp base deep green and leave to dry. Apply a coat of black patinating wax and buff off the excess with a soft cloth. For a mottled effect on the top of the lamp base, dampen a pad of kitchen towel with white spirit and dab over the surface to lift some of the wax.

8 Stick the squares onto the base, alternating the direction of the bamboo imprint from horizontal to vertical. Vary the position of the gold area to create a random effect.

Try this PLASTER-RELIEF PICTURE

The technique of imprinting clay with a natural material is extremely effective (see the lamp base, pages 86–87), and can be used for a host of other decorative ideas. This plaster-relief picture is particularly attractive.

YOU WILL NEED

- Self-hardening clay
- Sprig of bamboo
- Rolling pin
- Cutting mat
- Knife
- Silicone adhesive
- Mount board

1 Roll out a piece of clay to about 13cm (5in). Lay a small branch of bamboo veins down in the clay and press into it with a rolling pin. Mark a 10cm (4in) square on the clay. Follow steps 3–7 on pages 22–23 to make a plaster tile with the bamboo imprint.

2 Cut bamboo leaves into squares and press in the microwave (see Techniques, page 16). Stick the squares onto a frame, alternating the direction of veins in the leaves, using the photograph, right, as a guide. Mount the tile on a piece of mount board using silicone adhesive and fit into the frame.

FRUIT COASTERS

Pineapple, guava, papaya and other **mouthwatering** fruits are now as much a part of summer as the more familiar apples, peaches and pears. And where better to place your glass of **summer** fruit punch than on a coaster that encases a slice of one of these **delicious** exotics. Make a set of identical coasters, or a mix-and-match selection of different varieties to set taste buds into action all year round.

Fruits such as papaya and kumquats will dry out in an hour or two in a low oven. However, craft shops also have more common dried sliced fruits such as oranges and lemons that are ready to use, and if you are lucky you may even find something more **unusual** such as pineapple or guava slices.

EXOTIC DELIGHTS

FRUIT COASTERS

YOU WILL NEED

- Dried pineapple slices or other fruit of your choice

- Popping corn and black peppercorns or other decorative items of your choice

- 8–10cm (3–4in) round plastic food container

- Scissors

- Petroleum jelly

- Measuring jug

- Crystal resin kit including measuring spoons

- Container for mixing

- Tweezers and cocktail stick or skewer

Tip

Clear plastic containers do not need to be smeared with petroleum jelly to repel the resin mix.

Trim the food container so that the sides are about 2.5cm (1in) high and smear the inside with a very thin layer of petroleum jelly. Pour a little water into it deep enough to cover the fruit slice of your choice. Now pour the water from the container into a measuring jug to find the total quantity of resin required to make a coaster.

You will need to mix about 1/3 of this quantity of resin to begin with. A typical coaster uses 90ml (3fl oz/3/8 cup) of resin, so you will need to mix only 30ml (1fl oz/1/8 cup) at this stage. Following the manufacturer's directions, mix two parts of the resin mix with 1 part of hardener in another container. Pour into the container and leave for 4–5 hours until it is almost set.

Lay the pineapple slice in the centre of the resin. Using the tweezers, drop a black peppercorn centrally in the area between the fruit and the edge. Place another one opposite and then two more in between.

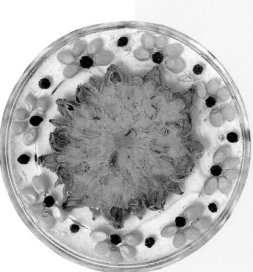

4 Place four more peppercorns in between the others so that there are eight in total. Use the tweezers to position a grain of popping corn on opposite sides of each peppercorn for 'petals'. Add another three to form a half flower shape around each peppercorn.

Finally, drop a peppercorn between each half flower. Leave to set for 3–4 hours. If the pieces begin to move about, manoeuvre them back into position with a cocktail stick or bamboo skewer. Once they are stable, mix the other ²/₃ of the resin. Avoid stirring too vigorously so that air bubbles are kept to a minimum, then pour into the container.

5

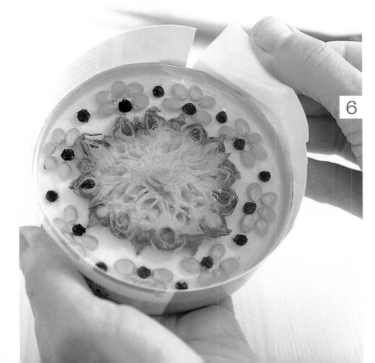

6 Leave the coaster to dry for at least 24 hours. To remove it, snip into the container and tear it away.

Tip

Allow plenty of time for this project because the resin needs to stiffen before and after the fruit is added. If you do act too quickly, the pieces will move out of position, but don't panic. You can push them gently back with a bamboo skewer.

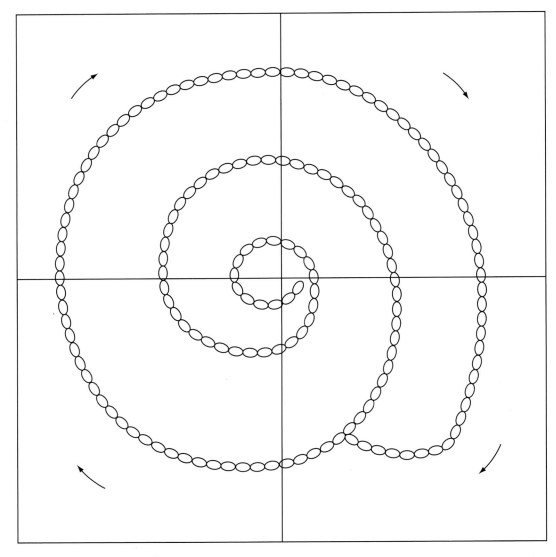

Miniature-shell Tiles
Snail
Page 20
Enlarge by 150%

Eggshell Mosaic
Page 70

**Japanese
Sushi Dishes**
Child Symbol
Page 66

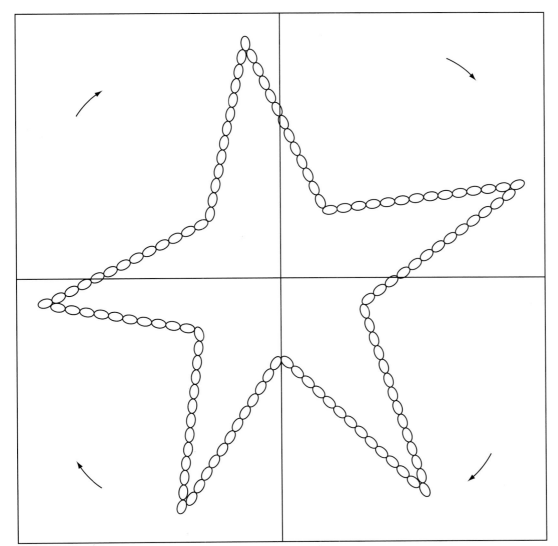

Miniature-shell Tiles
Starfish
Page 20
Enlarge by 150%

**Japanese
Sushi Dishes**
Woman Symbol
Page 66

**Japanese
Sushi Dishes**
Man Symbol
Page 66

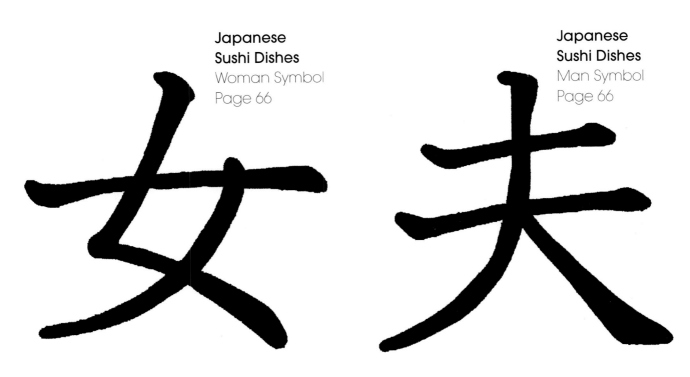

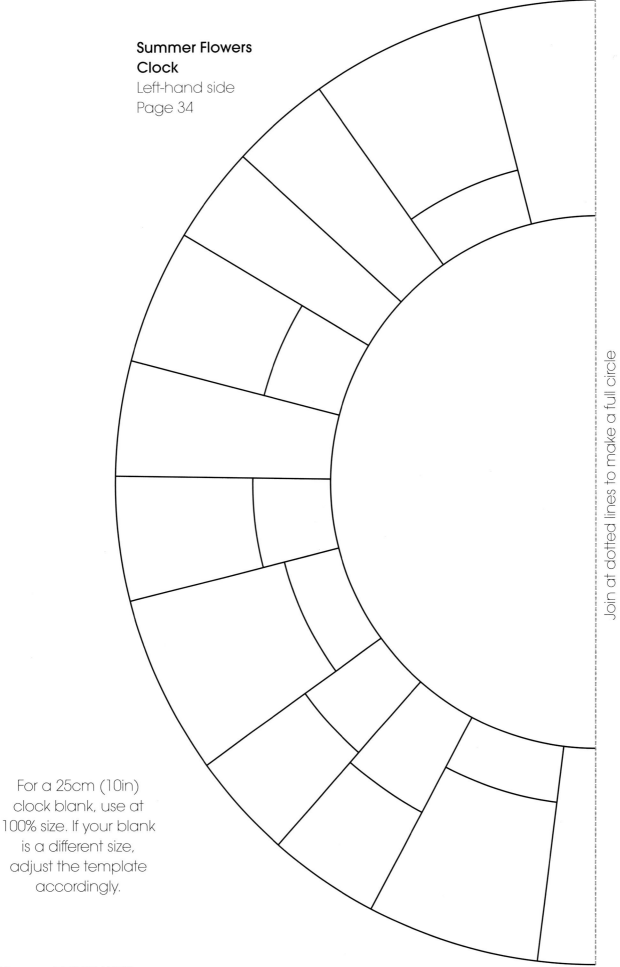

**Summer Flowers
Clock**
Left-hand side
Page 34

For a 25cm (10in)
clock blank, use at
100% size. If your blank
is a different size,
adjust the template
accordingly.

Join at dotted lines to make a full circle

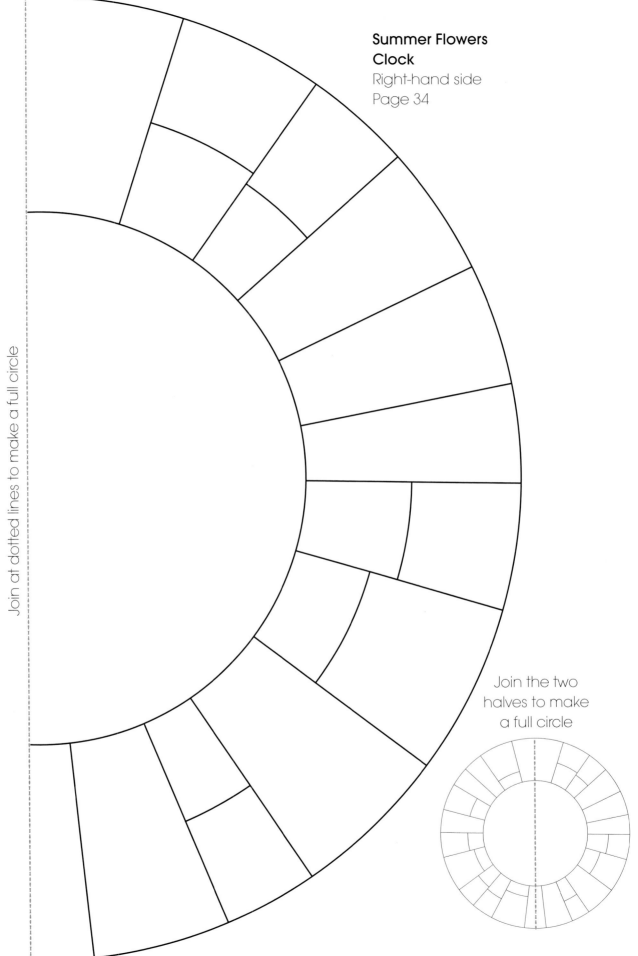

Summer Flowers Clock
Right-hand side
Page 34

Join at dotted lines to make a full circle

Join the two
halves to make
a full circle

Winter Leaf Tray
Page 40

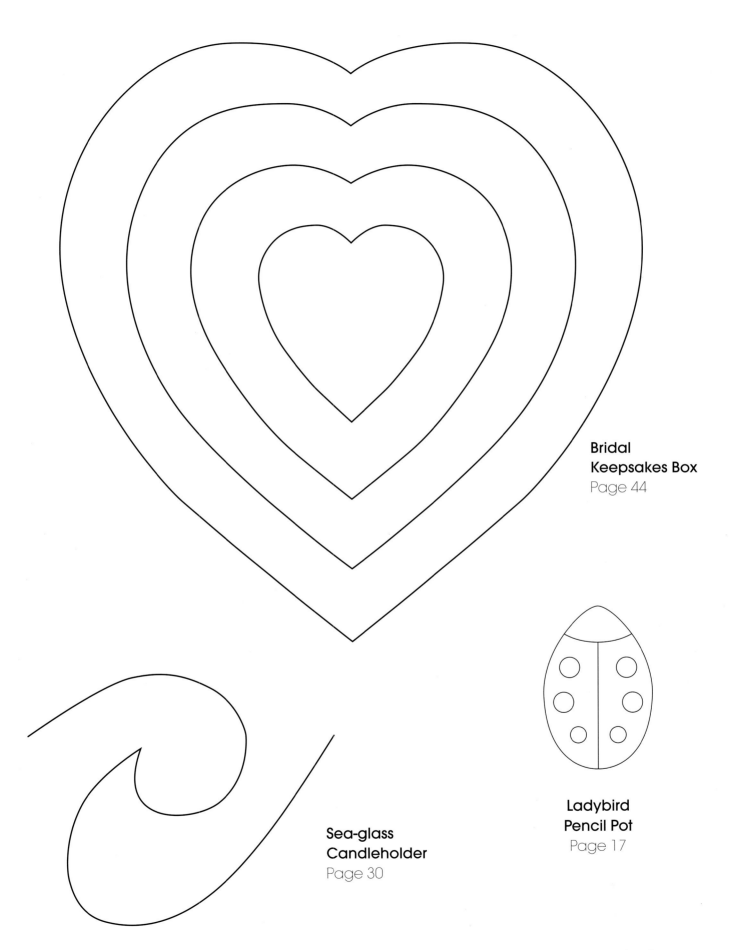

**Bridal
Keepsakes Box**
Page 44

**Sea-glass
Candleholder**
Page 30

**Ladybird
Pencil Pot**
Page 17

Decorative House Plaque

Numbers
Page 62

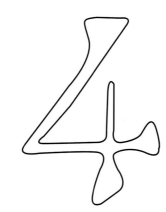
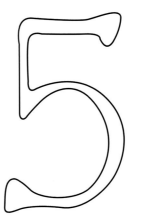
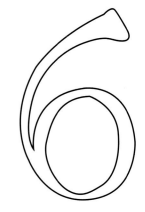

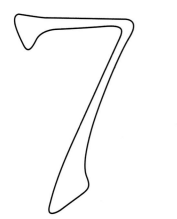
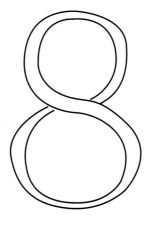
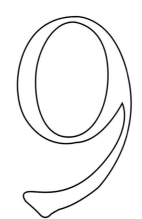
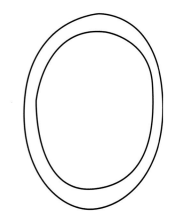

SUPPLIERS

Many suppliers offer a mail order service for overseas customers. Please contact them directly for more information

UK

The Canestore
Washdyke Cottage
1 Witham Road
Long Bennington
Newark NG23 5DS
tel: 01400 282 271
fax: 01400 281 103
email: enquiries@canestore.co.uk
www.canestore.co.uk
bamboo, willow bundles

Moira Clinch (mail order only)
64 Hackney Road
Matlock DE4 2PX
tel: 01629 581 026
Flower Dry (silica gel)

Croft Petals
The Old Dairy Barn
Dunmow Road
Beaushamp
Roding
Essex CM5 OPF
tel: 01279 876 757
fax: 01279 876 795
email: sales@croftpetals.co.uk
www.croftpetals.co.uk
pressed flowers, skeleton leaves, handmade papers and boxes

Eaton Seashells
tel: 0208 598 8321
fax: 0208 598 8321
email: eatonseashells@freenet.co.uk
www.eatonseashells.co.uk
shells

Elephant Furniture Ltd
(mail order available)
230 Tottenham Court Road
London W1T 7QQ
tel: 0207 637 7930
Brighton tel: 0127 373 1318
Bristol tel: 0117 929 7767
seashells, puspa pods, durian seed heads

L.J.Gibbs & Partners Limited
Mulberry House
Hewitts Road
Chelsfield
Kent BR6 7QS
tel: 01959 533 663
fax: 01959 534 082
www.ljgibbsandpartners.com
skeleton leaves and handmade paper

Goodness Direct
South March
Daventry
Northants NN11 4PH
tel: 0871 871 6611
fax: 01327 301 135
email: info@goodnessdirect.co.uk
www.goodnessdirect.co.uk
unshelled nuts

Hobbycraft stores
(mail order available)
tel: 0800 027 2387 for nearest store
tel: 01452 424 999
email: mgr22@stores.hobbycraft.co.uk
www.hobbycraft.co.uk
glass pebbles, seashells and starfish, papier mâché boxes, ribbon, self-hardening clay, dry foam shapes, general crafting materials

HomeCrafts Direct
PO Box 38
Leicester LE1 9BU
tel: 0116 269 7733
fax: 0116 269 7744
email: info@homecrafts.co.uk
www.homecrafts.co.uk
gel wax, plaster, mosaic grout, general crafting materials

Impress Cards and Craft Materials
Slough Farm
Westhall
Halesworth
Suffolk IP19 8RN
tel: 01986 781 422
fax: 01986 781 677
www.impresscards.com
microwave flower press, Mod Podge, silicone adhesive, pressed flowers

Janik
Brickfield Lane
Denbigh Road
Ruthin
Denbighshire LL15 2TN
tel: 0845 166 4911
fax: 0845 166 4912
email: sales@janik.co.uk
www.janik.co.uk
clock base and mechanism, wood plaque, pen pot, trinket box and other wooden blanks

Solstuf
PO Box 10597
Birmingham BS29 5XS.
tel: 0121 243 6067
www.solstuf.co.uk
dried rosebuds

Norpar Flowers
Navestock Hall
Navestock
Essex RM4 1HA
tel: 01277 374 968
fax: 01277 372 562
email: norparflowers@ukgatewaynet
www.norpar.co.uk
moss, lichen and bora berries

The Stamp Man
8a Craven Court
High Street
Skipton
North Yorkshire BD23 1DG
tel/fax: 01756 797 048
email: TheStampManUK@aol.com
www.thestampman.co.uk
wooden tray and album kit

Winter Flora Limited
Hall Farm
Weston
Beccles
Suffolk NR34 8TT
tel: 01502 713 346
email: info@winterflora.co.uk
www.winterflora.co.uk
willow bundles, pine cones and moss

USA

Beverly's Crafts & Fabrics
100 Cotton Lane
Souel, CA 95073
tel: 831 475 2954 / 831 475 1801
email: help@beverlys.com
www.save-on-crafts.com
dry-foam shapes including spheres, crystal resin

Columbia Pine Cones and Botanicals
PO Box 2077
Columbia, CA 95310
tel: 888 470 6989 / 209 533 0408
fax: 209 533 2515
email: Coneguys@aol.com
www.pinecones.com
acorns, pine cones, moss and lichen

Creative Papers Online
  Handmade Paper
PO Box 133
Pinckney, Michigan 48169
tel: 734 878 4895
toll-free: 800 727 3740
fax: 734 878 1738
email: sales@handmade-paper.us
www.handmade-paper.us
skeleton leaves, pressed flowers and handmade paper

Michael's Stores
8000 Bent Branch Dr.
Irving, TX 75063
tel: 800 642 4235
www.michaels.com
handmade paper, self-hardening clay, general craft supplies

Preserved Gardens Pressed Flowers
South East Michigan (internet only)
email: anne@preservedgardens.com
www.preservedgardens.com
pressed flowers, microwave flower press

Nature's Pressed
PO Box 212
Orem, UT 84059
tel: 801 225 1169 / 800 850 2499
fax: 801 225 1760
email: flowers@naturespressed.com
www.naturespressed.com
pressed flowers

Sanibel Seashells
905 Fitzhugh St
Sanibel, Fl 33957
tel: 239 472 1603
fax: 239 395 1525
email: ssi@seashells.com
sea-glass chips, seashells and starfish

ToleWood
1570 E. River Road
Olean, NY 14760
Tel/fax 716 372 3256
email: rdy2pnt@ToleWood.com
www.tolewood.com
wooden plaques

Winter Woods
701 Winter Woods Dr
PO Box 111
Glidden, WI 54527
tel: 800 541 4511 / 715 264 4892
fax: 715 264 4893
email: wwoods@centurytel.net
www.winterwoods.com
pine cones, moss, lichen and so on

ABOUT THE AUTHOR

Dorothy Wood is a talented and prolific craft maker and author. Since completing a course in Advanced Embroidery and Textiles at Goldsmith's College, London, she has written fifteen craft books and contributed to another twenty-three on all kinds of subjects. Dorothy also contributes to several well-known craft magazines, including *Crafts Beautiful*, and is the author of the best-selling *Simple Glass Seed Beading*, her first book published by David & Charles. Dorothy lives in the small village of Osgathorpe, Leicestershire, UK.

ACKNOWLEDGMENTS

I would like to thank the following companies for so generously supplying materials for this book: Hobbycraft, House of Marbles, Parlane International, Impress Cards, Croft Petals, Pébéo, LJ Gibbs and Partners, Woodware Toys and Gifts, Janik, Norpar Flowers and Winter Woods.

Thanks to the editorial team who made such a great job of putting the book together – Cheryl, Ali, Jennifer and Betsy. Thanks to Simon Whitmore for his really excellent photography and Lisa who has come up with such a superb book design.

Finally thanks to Jo and Bill Haldane for their hospitality and the use of their beautiful house in Devon for the photography.

INDEX